I Will Sprout

A SELF REFLECTION JOURNAL
FOR TEENAGERS

THE Resiliency PUBLISHING HOUSE

www.resiliencyhouse.org

This Journal Belongs To

Name: ....

Date: ....

CONTENTS

Before You Begin

You are always in control of what you write.

You may skip pages.

You may write a little or a lot.

You may stop at any time.

There is no right or wrong way to use this journal.

"You are enough just as you are."

— Maya Angelou

Dear Teenager,

The world can feel loud, confusing, and full of chaos.

Sometimes it feels like you're standing
right in the middle of it.

Or worse yet, when things feel heavy, it
can seem like you are the cause of it.

But that is not true.

You are not the problem.

Inside of you is the power to
grow, to change, and to do

meaningful things in this world.

Never forget that.

Are you ready to unleash it?

May this journal be a safe place to learn who
you are and who you are becoming.

Section 1

MY INNER SELF

*"The privilege of a lifetime
is being who you are."*

— Joseph Campbell

Who I am really am:

....

....

....

....

....

....

....

....

....

....

....

....

....

....

....

How I would describe who I am really am inside:

_____

_____

_____

_____

_____

_____

_____

_____

_____

_____

_____

_____

_____

_____

_____

_____

Qualities that I love about myself:

....

....

....

....

....

....

....

....

....

....

....

....

....

....

....

....

Section 2

WHAT I WISH OTHERS UNDERSTOOD ABOUT ME

"Be yourself; everyone else is already taken."

— Oscar Wilde

Something people often misunderstand about me:

What helps me feel heard:

When someone respects my boundaries, it feels like:

A sentence I wish I could say out loud:

....

....

....

....

....

....

....

....

....

....

....

....

....

....

....

....

Section 3

MY STRENGTHS

"*Our greatest glory is not in never falling,
but in rising every time we fall.*"

— Confucius

A strength I know I have:

A strength others have noticed in me:

A time I kept going even when things were hard:

....

....

....

....

....

....

....

....

....

....

....

....

....

....

....

....

Something I'm proud of—even if it seems small:

....

....

....

....

....

....

....

....

....

....

....

....

....

....

....

Section 4

MY CHALLENGES

"*I am not what happened to me,*
I am what I choose to become."

— Carl Jung

A difficult experience that I've had to cope with:

....

....

....

....

....

....

....

....

....

....

....

....

....

....

....

....

....

When the memory of this event shows up, my body feels:

....

....

....

....

....

....

....

....

....

....

....

....

....

....

....

....

What helps even a little:

What I wish people understood about this:

Section 5

WHEN CHALLENGES BECOME STRENGTHS

"Character cannot be developed in ease and quiet. Only through experience of trial and suffering can the soul be strengthened."

— Helen Keller

How can I use what I've been through to treat myself with kindness and help others?

If my future child went through a similar experience, what would I do for them or say to them to make them feel better?

....

....

....

....

....

....

....

....

....

....

....

....

....

....

....

....

Section 6

HOPES & MEANING

*"The future belongs to those who believe
in the beauty of their dreams."*

— Eleanor Roosevelt

Something that matters to me:

How I want to *feel* in my life:

....

....

....

....

....

....

....

....

....

....

....

....

....

....

....

....

Goals I hope to accomplish:

....

....

....

....

....

....

....

....

....

....

....

....

....

....

....

....

One small difference I'd like to make:

A hope I can hold gently:

Section 7

PEOPLE THAT I LOVE AND VALUE

"Try not to become a person of success, but rather try to become a person of value."

— Albert Einstein

Someone I love and admire:

....

....

....

....

....

....

Insert photo here

....

....

....

....

....

....

....

....

....

Qualities I admire most about them:

How I can imitate those qualities and become like the beautiful person I see in them:

....

....

....

....

....

....

....

....

....

....

....

....

....

....

....

Someone I love and admire:

....

....

....

....

....

....

| Insert photo here |

....

....

....

....

....

....

....

....

....

....

Qualities I admire most about them:

How I can imitate those qualities and become like the beautiful person I see in them:

....

....

....

....

....

....

....

....

....

....

....

....

....

....

....

....

Someone I love and admire:

....

....

....

....

....

....

Insert photo here

....

....

....

....

....

....

....

....

....

....

Qualities I admire most about them:

....

....

....

....

....

....

....

....

....

....

....

....

....

....

....

....

....

How I can imitate those qualities and become like the beautiful person I see in them:

....

....

....

....

....

....

....

....

....

....

....

....

....

....

....

Someone I love and admire:

....

....

....

....

....

....

Insert photo here

....

....

....

....

....

....

....

....

....

....

Qualities I admire most about them:

How I can imitate those qualities and become like the beautiful person I see in them:

....

....

....

....

....

....

....

....

....

....

....

....

....

....

....

Someone I love and admire:

....

....

....

....

....

....

Insert photo here

....

....

....

....

....

....

....

....

....

....

....

Qualities I admire most about them:

How I can imitate those qualities and become like the beautiful person I see in them:

....

....

....

....

....

....

....

....

....

....

....

....

....

....

....

....

Write a letter to yourself

Dear

I want you to know...

○ You are enough exactly as you are.

○ Your feelings matter.

○ What you've been through does not define your worth.

○ You are not weak for needing support.

○ You don't have to be perfect to be loved.

○ You are learning, growing, and doing the best you can.

○ You are stronger than you realize.

○ You are allowed to rest.

○ You are allowed to hope.

○ You are allowed to make mistakes.

○ Learning from your mistakes makes you beautiful.

Write your own affirmations here:

Date ....

Dear ....

I want you to know that... ....

✍

✍

✍

✍

✍

✍

✍

✍

✍

✍

✍

✍

✍

✍

✍

Write your own affirmations here:

Date ....

Dear ....

...... I want you to know that... ....

✍

✍

✍

✍

✍

✍

✍

✍

✍

✍

✍

✍

✍

✍

✍

Write your own affirmations here:

Date

Dear

I want you to know that...

Write your own affirmations here:

Date _____

Dear _____

_____ I want you to know that..._____

✍

✍

✍

✍

✍

✍

✍

✍

✍

✍

✍

✍

✍

✍

Daily Reflections

"We cannot change the cards we are dealt, just how we play the hand."

— Randy Pausch

Daily Reflection

Date:

Daily Reflection

Date:

Daily Reflection

Date: ....

....

....

....

....

....

....

....

....

....

....

....

....

....

....

....

Daily Reflection

Date:

Daily Reflection

Date:

Daily Reflection

Date:

Daily Reflection

Date:

Daily Reflection

Date:

Daily Reflection

Date:

Daily Reflection

Date: ....

Daily Reflection

Date:

Daily Reflection

Date:

Daily Reflection

Date: ....

Daily Reflection

Date:

Daily Reflection

Date: ....

Daily Reflection

Date:

Daily Reflection

Date: ....

....

....

....

....

....

....

....

....

....

....

....

....

....

....

....

Daily Reflection

Date:

Daily Reflection

Date:

Daily Reflection

Date:

Daily Reflection

Date: ....

Daily Reflection

Date:

Daily Reflection

Date: ....

Daily Reflection

Date:

Daily Reflection

Date:

Daily Reflection

Date:

Daily Reflection

Date:

Daily Reflection

Date:

Daily Reflection

Date:

Daily Reflection

Date:

Daily Reflection

Date:

Daily Reflection

Date:

Daily Reflection

Date: ....

....

....

....

....

....

....

....

....

....

....

....

....

....

....

Daily Reflection

Date:

Daily Reflection

Date:

Daily Reflection

Date:

Daily Reflection

Date:

Daily Reflection

Date: ....

Daily Reflection

Date:

Daily Reflection

Date:

Daily Reflection

Date:

Daily Reflection

Date:

Daily Reflection

Date:

Daily Reflection

Date:

Daily Reflection

Date:

Daily Reflection

Date:

Daily Reflection

Date:

Daily Reflection

Date: ....

Daily Reflection

Date: ....

Daily Reflection

Date:

Daily Reflection

Date:

Breathing & Grounding Exercises

Use these pages anytime you need to slow down, reset, or feel more grounded.

Slow Breathing

○ Breathe in through your nose for 4 seconds.

○ Hold for 2 seconds.

○ Breathe out through your mouth for 6 seconds.

○ Repeat 3-5 times.

○ You are safe in this moment.

5-4-3-2-1 Grounding

○ 5 things you can see

○ 4 things you can feel

○ 3 things you can hear

○ 2 things you can smell

○ 1 thing you can taste

Feet on the Floor

○ Place both feet flat on the floor.

○ Press them down gently.

○ Notice the support beneath you.

○ Take 3 slow breaths.

Hand on Heart

○ Place one hand on your chest.

○ Breathe slowly and gently.

○ Say quietly to yourself:

○ "I am doing the best I can."

One Sentence Reset

○ Write one sentence about how you feel right now.

○ That sentence is enough.

○ You can stop here.

Dear Teenager,

Sometimes you acted out because you wanted to be seen.
Because you wanted love.
Because you wanted attention and connection.

And that is okay.

Wanting love does not make you bad.
Wanting attention does not make you broken.

It makes you human.

You are not a bad kid.
You are a normal teenager learning how to survive, feel, and grow.

You are and will be okay.

Continue growing into the wonderful person you are.

With love,
The Resiliency Publishing House